CONTENTS

© A.R.E. Publishing, Inc. 2000
Springfield, New Jersey
www.behrmanhouse.com

ISBN-10: 0-86705-137-X
ISBN-13: 978-0-86705-137-7

LIFE IS A JOURNEY.

We often think of a journey as traveling from one place to another. Yet, when we say "Life is a journey," we mean something else. We mean traveling through a lifetime of experiences and events. Our "road of life" can be straight and smooth at times, and rocky, crooked, and bumpy at other times. But since it's our lifetime, it should certainly be interesting.

Your life is a journey through time.

It begins at your _____ and ends at your _____.

LIFE IS ALSO A CYCLE.

Special events mark our progress as we travel along the road of life. These events form a cycle for each person, like a wheel turning from birth to childhood to adulthood to old age to death.

In this book we will explore the events that make up the Jewish life cycle journey.

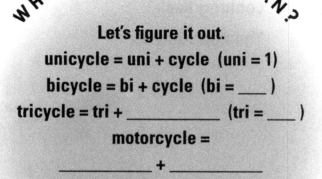

WHAT DOES CYCLE MEAN?

Let's figure it out.

unicycle = uni + cycle (uni = 1)

bicycle = bi + cycle (bi = ____)

tricycle = tri + _____ (tri = ____)

motorcycle =

_____ + _____

You get the picture! "Cycle" means

_____

2

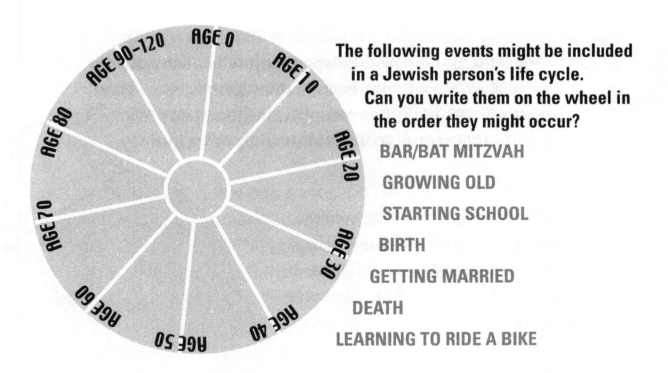

The following events might be included in a Jewish person's life cycle.

Can you write them on the wheel in the order they might occur?

BAR/BAT MITZVAH

GROWING OLD

STARTING SCHOOL

BIRTH

GETTING MARRIED

DEATH

LEARNING TO RIDE A BIKE

Our cycles are all similar in some ways and different in others. What are some events that occur in each and every person's life cycle?

_____

_____

What are some events that might occur in one person's life cycle but not in another's?

_____

_____

How many times does each person experience his/her own life cycle? _____

That's what I always say — you only go around once.

WHAT IS A LIFE CYCLE?

A TRAVEL GUIDE This book is like a travel guide. It's the kind of book you'd look at before taking a journey to a place you've never been. In these pages, we'll travel along the road of life — your life, the life of any Jew — and do some learning and sightseeing as we journey.

ON A MAGIC CARPET RIDE
Our mode of transportation will be a magic carpet. It's magic because it lets us fly back in time to your birth, and forward in time to leaving home and being an adult, and even to the end of life.

Our flying carpet will stay low to the ground. That way, we'll be able to chat with other travelers — people who, like you, are journeying along the road of life. And we'll also be able to get a good look at the landmarks along the way.

Customize your magic carpet by decorating it with colors, borders, and designs.

LANDMARKS The landmarks we'll explore are significant stops along the Jewish life cycle journey. The biggest ones are Brit Milah or Brit Bat, Bar or Bat Mitzvah, marriage, and death. We'll visit some smaller landmarks as well, such as Consecration and Confirmation.

Maybe you've noticed a problem. Maybe you're thinking, "The journey is different for each person. For example, some people never get married, and others get married more than once. And what if we visit the landmarks in a different order? My Grandma just had her Bat Mitzvah ceremony last year!"

WHAT IS A LIFE CYCLE?

You're absolutely right. In our real life cycle journeys, not all of us will visit all the landmarks in this book. That's what our magic flying carpet is for. Our carpet will take us to all the landmarks — marriage, divorce, conversion — so that we can learn about all of them, even those we may not end up "visiting" in our own individual lives.

BETWEEN THE LANDMARKS

In addition to the landmarks at which we'll be stopping, there will also be times when we're just traveling along our road — "Being a Child," for example, or "Old Age." These stretches of road are not unique to the Jewish journey; every person in every culture experiences them. As Jewish travelers, though, we'll find that our tradition has teachings and views on these times, as well as the "landmark" times. We're Jewish not only at our Brit or our Bat Mitzvah, or at our wedding or our funeral — **we're Jewish every day!**

WHY DO JEWS MAKE A BIG DEAL ABOUT LIFE CYCLE EVENTS?

Every culture has its own ways of celebrating life's changes and passages. Jews mark these important times using rituals and customs that connect us with other Jews across space and time. Jewish practices also help us to appreciate the significance of big changes in our lives. Finally, observing Jewish life cycle customs allows us to share these times with our family and friends — the good times as well as the bad.

Who would you like to connect with across space?

_____

_____

_____

Who would you like to connect with across time?

_____

_____

_____

ORIENTING OURSELVES ON THE MAP

Before we begin our journey, let's look at where we're going.

Of course, none of us — not even the wisest and cleverest of us — knows how long our life will be, or what will happen to us. Yet, we don't let that stop us from wondering, hoping, and dreaming about our future.

Can you fill in some features on your own road of life? Use one color for things that have already happened, and another color for hopes and dreams for the future. Draw a star to show where you are right now.

Birth

Death

Birth

Brit Bat/ Brit Milah

Being a Child

Bar/Bat Mitzvah

Confirmation

Growing Up

Leaving Home

Conversion

Marriage

Being an Adult

Divorce

Growing Old

Death/ Mourning

WHAT IS A LIFE CYCLE?

SOME THINGS YOU'LL FIND IN THIS BOOK:

 Vocabulary. Every good traveler learns to speak the "language of the land," at least enough to get around.

 As we noted before, the road isn't always straight and smooth. DETOURS occur when we go off the main road and explore what happens when a life journey takes an unpredictable turn.

 Here, just as the name says, we'll examine different Jewish customs, past and present, that relate to various parts of the journey.

 This signpost points out a commandment or good deed associated with a landmark or other part of the journey.

 This signals a chance for you to think about and/or record **your** feelings and thoughts about what you're learning.

 Experienced tour guides appear along the way to share advice or information. These guides may be famous Rabbis or teachers, or they may be "regular folks" who've been there already.

I'm Millie the Maven. A *maven* is an expert, and, believe me, I'm an expert in just about everything Jewish. You'll find me popping up here and there to put in my two cents.

WHAT IS A LIFE CYCLE?

READY-TO-GO CHECKLIST

To make sure you're ready to leave on the life cycle journey,
check the box that best fits each statement below.

	agree	disagree	not sure
1. Life is a journey.	❏	❏	❏
2. A cycle is a wheel that keeps turning and turning.	❏	❏	❏
3. Everyone's Jewish life journey happens in exactly the same way.	❏	❏	❏
4. Every culture has its own rituals for celebrating life's changes and passages.	❏	❏	❏
5. Celebrating Jewish life cycle events allows us to connect with other Jews across space and time.	❏	❏	❏

Your magic carpet is waiting at the curb!
But before you leave, complete this form:

MAGIC CARPET FLYER'S LICENSE

LEARNER'S PERMIT

I agree to READ and LEARN
before I
A. answer the questions or
B. do the fun activities.

Signed _____

Date _____

MY PICTURE

Your life cycle journey will begin, of course, with **birth**. Have a great trip!

8

It's a girl! It's a boy! Mazal Tov! Congratulations!

Birth or adoption is a time for **brachot** (blessings).
The **Shehecheyanu** is a great blessing for all happy events.
Let's learn it.

Moving On

בָּרוּךְ אַתָּה יְיָ אֱלֹהֵינוּ מֶלֶךְ הָעוֹלָם
שֶׁהֶחֱיָנוּ וְקִיְּמָנוּ וְהִגִּיעָנוּ לַזְּמַן הַזֶּה.

Baruch Atah Adonai Elohaynu Melech HaOlam
Shehecheyanu v'Keeyamanu v'Higeeyanu LaZ'man HaZeh.

Blessed are You, Adonai, God the universe, Who has kept us alive,
watched over us, and enabled us to reach this season.

CUSTOMS

Do you remember
the last time you said the
Shehecheyanu?

An ancient custom tells us to plant
a cedar tree when a boy is born,
and a cypress tree when a girl is
born. When the children grow up
and get married, branches from
these trees are used to make the
chupah (wedding canopy).

Word Guide

Brachah – Blessing
Brachot – Blessings
Shalom Zachar (for a boy)/
Shalom N'kayvah (for a girl) –
   The first Erev Shabbat (Friday night)
   after a baby is born, guests
   assemble in the home to sing
   songs and discuss Torah as a
   joyful welcome to the baby.

Would you believe there is no special blessing for childbirth?

Can you make up a blessing that parents might say
on the occasion of the birth of their child?

Blessed are You, Adonai, God of the universe, Who _____

_____

_____

_____

_____

If a new baby could talk, what blessing might he or she create?

Blessed are You, Adonai, God of the universe, Who _____

_____

_____

_____

_____

CUSTOMS

Some people believe that a new baby needs to
be protected from evil spirits, especially from Lilith
(Adam's first wife, according to folklore), who tries to
steal babies.

Some customs believed to protect the child include:

- Tying garlic to the baby's crib
- Tying a red thread on the crib
- Drawing a chalk circle around the bed

EVERYONE HAS A NAME.

How could we function if we didn't have names?
For Jews, names are important not only because they're useful,
but because they have meanings!

The forms below ask for information about your Jewish and your secular
name. You might need to ask your parents for help in completing them.

My Jewish name (Hebrew or Yiddish) is _____

ben/bat _____

☐ **I was named after someone with the same name.**

☐ **I was named after someone with the same initial letter.**

Who? _____

☐ **I was named after a famous person.**

Who? _____

Why? _____

☐ **My parents just liked my name for its sound or its meaning.**

My name means _____

It reminded my parents of _____

Ashkenazic Jews memorialize a
deceased (dead) relative by giving
a child the same name or a name
that starts with the same initial.
Sephardic Jews name their
children after living relatives as a
way of honoring them.

Do you
know any
Jewish people
with "Jr." after
their name?

My secular name is _____

❑ **I was named after someone with the same name.**

❑ **I was named after someone with the same initial letter.**

Who? _____

❑ **I was named after a famous person.**

Who? _____

Why? _____

❑ **My parents just liked my name for its sound or its meaning.**

My name means _____

It reminded my parents of _____

Check the appropriate box (or boxes) below.
Then fill in the lines next to each checked box.

Write the names here.

My Jewish and secular names . . .	Jewish	Secular
❑ are exactly the same.	_____	_____
❑ are almost the same.	_____	_____
❑ share the same initial letter.	_____	_____
❑ share the same meaning.	_____	_____
❑ are completely different!	_____	_____

More practices to avert evil spirits:

• **Some Jews won't buy or arrange anything for a new baby until after the baby is born.**

• **Some won't tell the name of a baby boy until the circumcision.**

Tour Guides

ADAM

> **Remember the story of Creation in the Torah? You may recall that God asked me, Adam, to name all the animals. I felt honored and powerful, and I took my job very seriously. I tried to give each animal a name that truly expressed its essence.**

Have you ever named a doll or a toy?
Have you ever named a living creature?

DOLL/TOY/CREATURE	NAME	REASONS FOR NAME
_____	_____	_____
_____	_____	_____
_____	_____	_____
_____	_____	_____

Now imagine you have twin babies to name —
a boy and a girl! (Mazal tov!) Look back at some of
the reasons for choosing a name.

	BOY	GIRL
A Jewish name I would choose	_____	_____
and why	_____	_____
A secular name I would choose	_____	_____
and why	_____	_____

CHECK IN

Do you think a person's name can affect what they do
and become in life?
Can a person's name affect how others treat him or her?
Have you ever wanted to change your name?

In the Torah, God tells Abraham to circumcise himself and all the males of his household. This was to be a sign of the covenant between God, Abraham, and all of Abraham's descendants (the Jewish people).

Moving On

To "enter the covenant" means to become a Jew.

When Abraham's son Isaac was eight days old, Abraham circumcised him. Ever since, Jews have circumcised their baby boys at eight days.

Word Guide

Bat – (Hebrew) Daughter

Brit (or *bris*) – Covenant, contract, agreement

Brit Bat or *Simchat Bat* – Ceremony welcoming a daughter into the covenant

Circumcision – Ritual removal of the foreskin, a piece of skin covering the tip of the penis

Covenant – Solemn agreement

Kisay shel Eliyahu – Elijah's chair. A chair is placed for Elijah the prophet, who is a guest of honor at every Brit Milah.

Milah – Circumcision

Mohel (pronounced "moil" in Yiddish) – A person who is trained to perform Brit Milah

Pidyon HaBen – Redemption of the Firstborn

Sandak – Person honored with holding the baby boy during the Milah (often a grandfather or other male relative)

Seudat Mitzvah – A meal celebrating the completion of a mitzvah — in this case, the mitzvah of bringing a child into the covenant

Wimpel – Long, decorated strip of fabric that is used to wrap the baby. This might later be used to wrap the Torah at a family life cycle ceremony.

Traditionally, while a Jewish baby boy had a **Brit Milah**, the welcome for a Jewish baby girl was her naming. She would be named in synagogue during a regular service on the first Shabbat following her birth.

Today, there's also a Jewish ceremony to welcome a girl into the covenant. It's called **Brit Bat** or **Simchat Bat**. Since this is a fairly new ritual created by liberal Jews, there aren't any rules for what such a ceremony includes. It can contain some of the important parts of a Brit Milah ceremony . . . but not all of them!

Ask one of your parents to help you complete the activity below. Then interview him/her in detail about your covenant experience as a baby (see next page).

	BRIT MILAH	BRIT BAT	WHAT WAS MY EXPERIENCE?
When it happens	8 days	any time after birth	_____
A baby is welcomed as a part of the Jewish people	yes	yes	_____
Includes circumcision	yes	no	_____
Includes blessings for the baby to have Torah, chupah (wedding canopy), and ma'aseem toveem (good deeds) in his or her life	yes	yes	_____
Includes Kiddush over wine, which is always part of a joyful and holy Jewish celebration	yes	yes	_____
Is followed by a festive meal	yes	yes	_____

PARENT INTERVIEW:

Did I have a **Brit Milah** or a **Brit Bat**, or similar welcoming ceremony?

❑ yes   ❑ no

(If **yes**, keep going. If **no**, skip to the box at the bottom of the page.)

How old was I? _____

Where was the ceremony held? _____

Who was there? _____

_____

What happened there? _____

_____

_____

How did you feel that day? _____

_____

_____

What did this ceremony mean to our family? _____

_____

_____

Do you think it's important for a baby to be welcomed into the Jewish people? ❑ **yes**   ❑ **no**

Why or why not? _____

_____

_____

_____

What would you add to the celebration? _____

_____

_____

ELIJAH

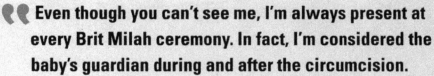

Even though you can't see me, I'm always present at every Brit Milah ceremony. In fact, I'm considered the baby's guardian during and after the circumcision.

Can you think of two other times you might sense my presence? I'll give you a hint: on one holiday, you pour me a glass of wine and hold the door open for me. It's the holiday of _____.
And at the end of Shabbat every week, you sing a song about me. That ceremony is called _____.

ELIJAH'S CHAIR

Can you decorate my special chair?
You might want to use symbols of the other
covenants described in the Torah:

After the flood, God places a _____ in the sky as a promise never again to destroy the earth by flood.

God gives the _____ at Mount Sinai. The Jews accept the Torah, and God promises to be their God.

The Jews promise that they and their descendants will keep _____ holy. They get a day of rest in exchange for remembering and honoring God's creation.

DECORATE THIS WIMPEL. Use letters of the alef-bet to symbolize the importance of Jewish education in a child's life. The letters also remind us of the _____ scroll, which might be wrapped by the wimpel.

CUSTOMS

After a Brit Milah, the baby might be placed in his cradle along with a Chumash (Torah in book form). His parents would then say, "May this child fulfill what is written in this book!"

DETOUR

Q: What if the eight-day old baby boy is sick?

A: His Brit Milah will be postponed until he has recovered.

MITZVAH STOP

It's a mitzvah to attend a Brit Milah. Therefore, it's also a mitzvah to invite a lot of guests to the ceremony.

TALKING HEADS: A TOUR GUIDES' FORUM

Abraham: You know that I'm famous for my faith in God. My faith was immense! So, when God told me and all the men in my household that we had to be circumcised, we didn't hesitate, even though we knew it would be painful. I was even ready to sacrifice my own son, my Isaac, if that was what Adonai wanted! Now we have a reminder on our bodies of our commitment to one God. It's a reminder of the way God wants us to behave in the world.

The new father: My son's Brit was an awesome experience for me. My father sat in Elijah's chair, right there in my living room, holding my little eight-day-old son, as the mohel performed the Milah. I suddenly sensed that we are links in a chain that stretches for centuries in two directions — backward and forward from this moment. I hope the chain will continue to reach far into the future.

The new mother: I'm aware that Milah is a very important mitzvah, and I'm happy about welcoming our son into our wonderful Jewish tradition. Still, I was sad that my little tiny baby had to feel pain even for a second.

The baby: Actually, it did hurt, but only for a moment. I'm glad that the mohel was so quick! The next thing I knew I was drinking my first drops of sweet wine, and I started to feel better. Then I fell asleep!

You: Draw yourself here, and write your own thoughts on the ritual of Brit Milah or Brit Bat.

_____

_____

_____

ACROSS

3. _____ Zachar or Nekayvah — special first Shabbat for a baby boy or girl

6. A Jewish name may be _____ or Yiddish.

7. Wish for every baby: Torah, Chupah, and good _____s

8. I'm present at every Brit ceremony — even if you can't see me.

10. I'm a wrapper — for a baby today, for a Torah tomorrow.

11. Covenant (Hebrew)

12. _____ days old for a Brit Milah

14. Hebrew word for blessing (hint: it always starts with "Baruch")

DOWN

1. Tie me to the crib to ward off evil, but don't be surprised if my strong smell keeps baby awake!

2. To "enter the covenant" means to become a _____.

3. I have the honor of holding the baby at the Brit Milah.

4. I'm so good at what I do, the baby will hardly cry.

5. A commandment was done! This is the part where we celebrate like crazy!

9. Circumcision (Hebrew)

13. Redemption of the firstborn: Pidyon _____.

You're really getting the hang of this magic carpet! Speed up a little and we'll cruise right into childhood.

Adults sometimes look back fondly on childhood as a time when they had few or no responsibilities. Of course, most children do have some responsibilities. Do you?

My responsibilities at home include: _____

_____

_____

My responsibilities with regard to school include: _____

_____

_____

My Jewish responsibilities include: _____

_____

_____

Actually, our Jewish tradition tells us that children have one very important responsibility: to embark on a lifelong learning quest. The **Talmud** makes it clear that, although children are not required to follow the mitzvot until they become Bar or Bat Mitzvah, they are required to learn about the mitzvot — so that they'll know what to do later.

Word Guide

Talmud – A collection of Jewish laws and writings written by Rabbis during the first six centuries C.E.

Consecration – A modern ceremony held in a synagogue, usually on Simchat Torah, celebrating the beginning of a child's formal education (see Tour Guide, page 23)

BEING A CHILD

The Torah emphasizes that "you must teach your children." While a child's formal education begins when he or she goes to school, that same child's informal education begins just after birth!

Someone your age has already learned a staggering number of things. Fill in this chart to show a bit of what you've learned.

What I've learned	How old I was when I learned it, or "not yet"	Who taught me	Learned at school? yes or no
Recite the Shema	_____	_____	_____
Tie my shoes	_____	_____	_____
Read in Hebrew	_____	_____	_____
Multiplication tables	_____	_____	_____
Say "please" and "thank you"	_____	_____	_____
Ask the Four Questions at the Pesach Seder	_____	_____	_____
Be fair and kind to others	_____	_____	_____

Kids teach their parents a thing or two as well. Do you ever teach your parents?

I have taught my parents _____

_____

_____

_____

_____

Tour Guides
JUST A KID

Unscramble these words to fill in the blanks.

1 CRATCONNOISE*
2 DRETARENGINK
3 GANGOSUEY
4 MASTICH ROHAT
5 MAHIB
6 LORLCS
7 STAPNER

*See Word Guide on page 21.

" I remember my __ __ __ __ __ __ __ __ __ __ __ ceremony wa-a-ay back when I was starting Jewish school. Now I'm your age, but I was just in __ __ __ __ __ __ __ __ __ __ __ __ then! We were at the __ __ __ __ __ __ __ __ __ to celebrate the holiday of __ __ __ __ __ __ __ __ __ __ __ __ . All of us little kids were called up to the __ __ __ __ __ . We sang a little song we'd learned about the letters of the alef-bet. Then each of us was given a little tiny Torah __ __ __ __ __ __ all our own. I still have mine! All our __ __ __ __ __ __ __ were very proud. "

Word Guide

Upsherin (Yiddish, meaning to shear off) — Celebration of a Jewish child's first haircut

CUSTOMS

Upsherin is an interesting custom that dates back to sixteenth century Poland. It is still observed by many Jews today. A boy's first haircut usually takes place after his third birthday on the spring holiday of **Lag B'Omer**. Family and friends help with the cutting, leaving long the **payes** or **payot** (side curls). The family might weigh the cut-off hair and donate a comparable amount of money to **tzedakah**. The child might also receive his first **tallit katan** with **tzitzit** (ritual fringes), which he will then wear at all times.

Word Guide

Cheder (Yiddish, literally "room")
– Traditional Jewish elementary school

Rashi (1040-1105) – A famous teacher and Torah commentator. His helpful explanatory notes are traditionally studied alongside the Torah text.

Tour Guides

RASHI

" In my time, only the boys went to cheder to study with the Rabbi. The girls were expected to stay at home. Oh, they studied, but they also had to help with the housekeeping. Cooking, sewing, keeping kosher — these were their most important subjects. Not my daughters, though! I made sure they became outstanding scholars in Torah and Talmud, as educated as any boy.

Anyway, maybe you're wondering why students nearly always study my commentaries alongside the Torah and Talmud. You see, these wonderful and holy books can often be confusing. My comments help students understand what they're learning. "

Although Rashi's comments are written in Hebrew, they are printed in a different font known as Rashi script. Pretend you are a student at **cheder** just learning to read Rashi script. Can you find and underline the word for Jerusalem in the paragraph below?

ENGLISH	HEBREW	RASHI SCRIPT
Jerusalem	ירושלים	ירושלים

גילה לו מתחלה, שלא לטרבבו פתחום ותזוח דעתו עליו ותטרף. וכדי
לחבב עליו את המלוה וליתן לו שכר על כל דבור ודבור (שם ושס;ב"ר
שם ז): ארץ המריה. ירושלים. וכן בדברי הימים (ב ג:א) לבנות

We haven't seen any major landmarks for a while, but here comes a big one: **Bar/Bat Mitzvah**. And guess what? You become one at age 13 — whether you're ready or not!

Moving On

Tour Guides

JUDITH KAPLAN EISENSTEIN

❝ I was the first girl ever to celebrate becoming a Bat Mitzvah by reading a Torah portion in synagogue! That was in 1922. Before that, a girl might be given a special party at the time of Bat Mitzvah, but nothing more. My family was different! My father, Rabbi Mordecai Kaplan, believed that Jewish women should have the same rights and responsibilities as Jewish men. ❞

Word Guide

Bar Mitzvah (Son of the Commandment)

Bat Mitzvah (Daughter of the Commandment) — A Jewish 13-year-old; one who is expected to observe the commandments. Also, the ceremony which celebrates reaching this milestone.

Trope – Melodies used for chanting Torah and Haftarah

CHECK IN

Do you agree with Rabbi Kaplan? Why or why not?

_____

_____

_____

What is the position of your synagogue on this subject?

_____

_____

HOW WILL YOU CELEBRATE BECOMING A BAR OR BAT MITZVAH?

What will be expected of you?
How will you and your family prepare?

Each synagogue has its own guidelines or suggestions for how to mark this important occasion. Invite your Rabbi or Cantor to your class for an interview. Ask him or her how the following components of a Bar/Bat Mitzvah are treated in your community. Take notes and share with your family.

The Rabbis taught that a girl became responsible for the mitzvot at age 12 1/2. In this book, though, we will refer to the age for both girls and boys as 13.

ASK ABOUT:	Is it done here? What are the details? How will I prepare?
Which days of the week?	
Which service?	
Which prayers does child lead?	
Tallit ceremony	
Torah portion	
Haftarah	
Original readings or prayers	
Speeches and by whom	
Oneg or Kiddush	
Party	
Number of guests	

ANSWER THE FOLLOWING:
Preparing to become Bar/Bat Mitzvah is a whole lot of work just to get ready for one day!   ❑ True   ❑ False

That was a trick question! Yes, it's a lot of work, but it's not just for one day. Your Bar/Bat Mitzvah ceremony isn't the only time you'll use what you've learned. Look at the Bar/Bat Mitzvah Planner below and write your initials in the appropriate ovals.

I will need to:	I am already good at this.	I'll need to work on this.	This skill might be useful later in life.
1 **Read Hebrew**	⬭	⬭	⬭
2 **Learn prayers well enough to lead services**	⬭	⬭	⬭
3 **Learn to chant using trope**	⬭	⬭	⬭
4 **Write a speech dealing with a Torah portion**	⬭	⬭	⬭
5 **Organize my schedule in order to get all my studying done**	⬭	⬭	⬭
6 **Speak clearly before a big group of people**	⬭	⬭	⬭
7 **Write thank-you notes for any gifts I might receive**	⬭	⬭	⬭

CUSTOMS

During the Spanish Inquisition (fourteenth-fifteenth centuries), to be Jewish in Spain was a crime punishable by death. Still, thousands of Jews continued their Jewish practices in secret, many for generations. These "hidden Jews," or Conversos, kept their Jewish background a secret from their children until the children reached the age of Bar/Bat Mitzvah. Why do you think the parents chose thirteen as the best age to reveal this crucial information?

_____

_____

_____

DETOUR →

Q: What if a child has a disability that prevents him or her from being able to read a Torah or Haftarah portion? Can the child still celebrate Bar/Bat Mitzvah in a synagogue service?

A: Yes. The child is encouraged to do only as much as he or she can handle, even if it's just one prayer or a short speech. Our ancestors would allow a developmentally disabled child to fulfill the requirements by collecting wax to make candles for the synagogue. This was in accordance with the saying "Torah is light."

There's more than one way to become a "child of the commandment."

You could say that Bar/Bat Mitzvah is one BIG mitzvah stop: it's the moment you become responsible for doing all the commandments.

In addition, some families find that Bar/Bat Mitzvah can be a great time for fulfilling the mitzvah of giving tzedakah. Would you consider any of the following ways to use your celebration as an opportunity for giving?

	YES	NO	MAYBE
1 Doing a mitzvah project with your class or family as part of your preparation	❑	❑	❑
2 If you have a party, using centerpieces made out of packaged food products or toys or books, and then donating those to a shelter or school	❑	❑	❑
3 Asking guests to contribute to your favorite charity instead of giving you gifts	❑	❑	❑
4 Contributing some of your own gifts to tzedakah	❑	❑	❑

During a traditional Bar Mitzvah ceremony, the father recites: "Blessed is God, Who has freed me from the responsibility of this one." This means that the son is now responsible for his own moral decisions and actions.

At your thirteenth birthday, what sorts of moral decisions might you be ready to make for yourself?

_____

What decisions will you still leave up to your parents?

_____

GROWING UP

As you've just seen, Bar/Bat Mitzvah is not an ending, but a beginning. At thirteen, you'll have started the process of becoming fully responsible for yourself. For most people, that process will continue for a long time.

We call this part of the journey GROWING UP. During your teen years, you will encounter increasingly difficult decisions to make.

There are many people who can help you make such decisions — friends, parents, other family members, adult friends, teachers, Rabbis, doctors. Our sacred texts have also offered guidance to Jews over the centuries. Look at some of the decisions on the next page.

CONFIRMATION

The Confirmation ceremony is a relatively new custom that originated in the Reform Movement. The first one was held in 1810 in a synagogue in Kassel, Germany.

Confirmation is a ceremony in which a group of young women and men reaffirm their commitment to Judaism at about age sixteen. The ceremony most often takes place during Shavuot, the holiday celebrating the Jews' acceptance of the Torah at Mount Sinai.

Does your synagogue have a Confirmation ceremony? _____

At one time Confirmation was intended to replace Bar/Bat Mitzvah. What do you think of this idea? _____
_____
_____
_____

Why is Shavuot a particularly appropriate holiday during which to hold a Confirmation ceremony? _____
_____
_____

The kids on the left are facing decisions. The writings on the right offer Jewish perspective on the decisions. Draw lines to show the appropriate connections.

Find someone you can talk to . . . and use your common sense!

My friend wants me to start smoking. Should I?

"Honor your father and your mother." *(Exodus 19:12)*

Should I have a salad for lunch, or a can of soda?

"You shall not . . . make any tattoo marks upon you . . ." *(Leviticus 19:28)*

Should I get a tattoo?

". . . take good care of yourself . . ." *(Deuteronomy 2:4)*

Should I let my parents know what's going on in my life?

"It is forbidden to live in a city that does not have a vegetable garden." *(Palestinian Talmud)*

ACROSS

2. Lag B'Omer: a good holiday for a first _____ .
4. The Talmud warned against living in a city that doesn't have a vegetable _____ .
6. Ceremony marking the beginning of formal Jewish education
10. J.K. Eisenstein was the first person to celebrate this at a synagogue service.
11. Bar or Bat _____ = Child of the Commandment
12. "And you shall teach your _____ "
13. Newish ceremony for 16-year-olds

DOWN

1. Your informal _____ begins at birth.
3. If you learn the trope, you can _____ your Torah portion instead of just reading it.
5. Shavuot celebrates that "We got it!" at Mount Sinai. What did we get?
7. Age at which a Jew is responsible for the commandments
8. Those Big Big Books of Jewish learning: Torah and _____ .
9. Odd-looking Hebrew letter font

LEAVING HOME

When a grown child leaves home, it's a big step for the child (who isn't a child any more), and for the parents as well. Imagine a conversation between a parent and a grown child as the child is moving out for the first time.

Moving On

CHILD : I'm glad about _____

_____

_____

_____

I'm worried about _____

_____

_____

_____

On Shabbat and holidays, I will

_____

_____

_____

I'd like it if you would _____

_____

_____

_____

PARENT : I'm glad about _____

_____

_____

_____

I'm worried about _____

_____

_____

_____

On Shabbat and holidays, I will

_____

_____

_____

I'd like it if you would _____

_____

_____

_____

Don't be a stranger! Phone home once in a while!

For some people, this next stop is the **first** landmark on the Jewish life cycle journey.

It's **CONVERSION**. That's the name of the process by which people who aren't born Jewish become Jewish. It can take place at any age in a person's life.

Let's study the Word Guide, then explore this interesting landmark.

Word Guide

Beit Din (pronounced "bait deen") – A "court" of three learned people, at least one of whom is a Rabbi. The prospective convert is asked a variety of questions to test his or her knowledge of and commitment to Judaism.

Convert – A person who has converted to Judaism

Ger (masc.)/*Gioret* (fem.) – A convert

Jew-by-Choice – Yet another (and perhaps the most respectful) way to refer to someone who has converted to Judaism

Mikvah – Ritual bath. Immersion in the *mikvah* is part of the conversion process.

CUSTOMS

Some Rabbis follow a tradition of *discouraging* a person who approaches them for conversion. They do this three times. If the person returns a fourth time, the Rabbi will accept them to begin studying.

Why do you think a Rabbi would go through this process?

_____

_____

_____

Sorry, not this time!

Being Jewish — some people are born that way,
and others choose it for themselves.

Complete the table below to find out more about what
we choose for ourselves and what we don't.

Something about me	List or describe	I was born that way	Someone chose it for me	I chose (or choose) it for myself
		CHECK ONE		
Eye color	_____	❏	❏	❏
What I'm wearing today	_____	❏	❏	❏
Where I live	_____	❏	❏	❏
My school	_____	❏	❏	❏
My synagogue	_____	❏	❏	❏
What I eat for breakfast	_____	❏	❏	❏
My hobbies	_____	❏	❏	❏
My friends	_____	❏	❏	❏
My religion	_____	❏	❏	❏
My talents	_____	❏	❏	❏
My personality	_____	❏	❏	❏

What did you learn from this exercise? _____

_____

CONVERSION

Here's a mixed-up story about a person who becomes a
Jew-by-Choice. Can you put the story in the right order by
placing a number next to each part?

_____ **The person may have a formal ceremony marking the end of the
conversion process. He/she is given a Hebrew name, and is called
"son/daughter of Abraham our father and Sarah our mother."**

_____ **When the person has finished studying, he/she appears before a
Beit Din to be tested. He or she is approved by the Beit Din.**

_____ **The person is considered a Jew in every respect.**

_____ **As preparation for their ceremony, the person visits the mikvah to be
spiritually cleansed.**

_____ **A person approaches a Rabbi and says he/she would like to convert
to Judaism.**

_____ **After determining that the person is sincere, the Rabbi agrees that
he/she can begin learning what it means to be a Jew.**

_____ **If the person is a male who wasn't circumcised as a child,
he is circumcised.**

Interview someone who has converted to Judaism. Ask them:

Why did you convert? _____

_____

How old were you? _____

What was the most difficult part of the process? _____

_____

Tour Guides

RUTH

> I am probably the most famous gioret (Jew-by-Choice) in the Torah. There's a whole book named after me! I was a Moabite who married a Jew. When my husband died, I decided to stay by the side of his mother Naomi (my mother-in-law), rather than go back to my parents' home. I told Naomi, "Wherever you go, I will go, and wherever you stay, I will stay. Your people will be my people and your God will be my God." Eventually, I remarried and, believe it or not, King David was my great-grandson! I'm considered a hero for my commitment to the Jewish people.

DETOUR

Q: A baby whose birth parents are not Jewish is adopted by a Jewish couple. Is the baby automatically considered Jewish, or does he/she have to convert?

A: The baby has to convert! For a child, conversion has only two or three steps:
1. Immersion in the mikvah
2. Circumcision (for a boy)
3. Receiving a Hebrew name

CHECK IN

People who convert to Judaism have to pass a test, but people who are born Jewish do not. Do you think that is fair? Why or why not?

_____

_____

_____

_____

_____

It's a great day for cruising down the road on our carpet. But wait! Do you hear that music? It's coming from over there. Yes, it looks like a big party. IT'S A WEDDING! Let's stop and join in the celebration. First, though, we'd better consult our Word Guide so we'll know what's going on.

Moving On

Word Guide

Aufruf – A bride and groom are called to the Torah during Shabbat services in honor of their wedding.

Bedeken – The groom covers the bride's face with her veil just before the procession to the chupah.

Chupah – Marriage canopy. It's considered an honor for close friends and relatives to hold one of the poles.

Intermarriage – Marriage between a Jew and a non-Jew who hasn't converted

Ketubah – Document spelling out mutual obligations of marriage partners, signed at the wedding before proceeding to the chupah

Kiddushin – Betrothal ceremony. Once separate from the wedding, now the first part of a traditional wedding ceremony

Mikvah – Ritual bath. Traditionally, the bride immerses herself before her wedding. Orthodox women will continue to visit the mikvah once a month throughout their married life.

Nissuin – Second half of the wedding ceremony

Seudat Mitzvah – Festive meal celebrating the completion of a mitzvah — in this case, getting married

Shadchan (masc.)/***Shadchanit*** (fem.) – Matchmaker, marriage broker

Shidduch – Match (between a prospective bride and groom)

Sheva Brachot – The seven special blessings at a wedding

Tennaim – Conditions traditionally agreed to by the parents of the bride and groom, including the date and time of the wedding, the parents' financial commitments to the couple, dowry, and inheritance rights.

MARRIAGE

Men and women meet each other in various ways. Before modern times, though, marriages were most often arranged by a **shadchan** or **shadchanit** (professional matchmaker).

Pretend for a minute that you are a shadchan or shadchanit. You are an expert at putting brides and grooms together! You must consider many factors as you figure out whether a man and woman will be a good match for each other. Here's a page from your notebook. Look it over, and then answer the questions at the bottom of this page.

	BRIDE _SOPHIE_	GROOM _MAX_
Amount of Jewish knowledge	Speaks Hebrew	Studies Talmud
Family backgrounds	Ashkenazic	Sephardic
Keeping kosher and other food restrictions	Vegetarian	Kosher
How religious?	Reform	Orthodox
Height	5'7"	5'6"
Age	23	27
Hobbies	Hiking	Watching TV
Sense of humor	Jokes a lot	Rather serious
Wealth	Wealthy parents	Middle class

Do you think these two will be a good match? Why or why not?

_____

_____

Now be a matchmaker of a different sort. See if you can match the marriage customs and rituals (in the left-hand column) with the meanings behind them (in the right-hand column).
Write the letter of the correct meaning next to the custom or ritual.
HINT: Read all the customs before you start making matches.

_____ In days past, toasted grains and nuts were thrown; rooster and hen were part of the wedding procession.

_____ The couple fasts on the wedding day and doesn't eat until after the ceremony.

_____ At the aufruf, the groom (or couple) are showered with candy and raisins as they leave the bimah.

_____ The couple stands under a chupah.

_____ During the ceremony, the ring is slipped onto the index finger, not the ring finger.

_____ The groom places the veil over the bride's face just before the ceremony.

_____ The groom shatters a glass by stepping on it at the end of the ceremony.

_____ When the bride and groom arrive at the chupah, she walks around him three or seven times.

_____ In traditional communities, the celebration continues for a whole week, with parties each night when the Sheva Brachot are recited.

A. Some say a vein connects this finger directly to the heart.

B. Why not extend the wedding celebration to seven days — one day for each of the seven blessings?

C. Symbols of fertility

D. In the Torah, Rebekah covered her face with a veil before meeting Isaac. Later, Jacob was given Leah in marriage instead of Rachel, his chosen bride. If only he'd been allowed to see first who was behind the veil!

E. Wishes of sweetness and fruitfulness for the bride and groom

F. In medieval times, the circle was thought to be a protective shield that might ward off evil spirits.

G. Symbolizes the destruction of the Temple in Jerusalem, reminding us that marriages have both joyous and sad times.

H. Like a roof over their heads, it symbolizes the new home they will make together.

I. Like a mini-Yom Kippur, they atone for their sins to start a new life together.

MARRIAGE

Here's a helpful "scheduling list" which a Rabbi prepared for people who are planning a wedding. It lists the parts of the Jewish marriage process in their correct order. Unfortunately, the Rabbi left a few blanks in it. Can you fill them in?

GETTING READY

1. A man and woman meet and decide to get married. Traditionally, the match would be made by a _____.

2. The aufruf: In synagogue on the Shabbat before the wedding, friends throw _____ at the bride and groom.

3. The bride immerses herself in the _____.

BEFORE THE CEREMONY

4. The witnesses (and usually the bride and groom) _____ the ketubah.

5. In the ceremony known as_____, the groom puts the bride's veil over her face.

6. The bride and groom are escorted to stand under the _____.

7. The bride_____ the groom three or seven times.

CEREMONY PART 1: KIDDUSHIN

8. A _____ is exchanged with these words: "You are consecrated to me according to the faith of Moses and Israel."

9. The _____ is read out loud.

CEREMONY PART 2: NISSUIN

10. The Sheva _____ are sung or recited.

11. The couple drinks from a glass of _____.

12. The groom steps on a _____.

THE WEDDING FEAST

13. Eat, drink, dance, and celebrate! And don't forget to congratulate the _____ and_____.

Tour Guides

BAAL SHEM TOV

> ❝❝ From each person there rises a light that reaches straight to heaven. When two people find each other and get married, their streams of light join together into a single, brighter light! ❞❞

There are a lot of customs for marriage!

DETOUR ➦

Q: According to Jewish law, can a Jew marry anyone he or she chooses?

A: According to Jewish law, there are four types of people that a Jew is not allowed to marry:

1. Anyone in your family who is more closely related than a cousin
2. Someone who is already married
3. A non-Jew
4. Someone of the same sex

The first two are still held by all Jews today. As for the second two, *some* liberal Rabbis today will perform intermarriages and same-sex marriages.

CHECK IN ➤

If I were a Rabbi, I
❏ would   ❏ would not
perform intermarriages.
Why or why not?

_____

_____

If I were a Rabbi, I
❏ would   ❏ would not
perform same-sex marriages.
Why or why not?

_____

_____

So here we are in **ADULTHOOD**. God willing, this will be a nice, long part of our journey.

Adults have to make many choices about how to live their lives — choices about family, work, home, and community, and choices about how to be Jewish.

Moving On

It used to be that men and women had very different choices available to them. Complete the table below to see if this is still true today.

To whom are/were these choices available?	100 YEARS AGO		TODAY		Might *you* choose this as an adult?
	Men	Women	Men	Women	
Study Talmud	❏	❏	❏	❏	_____
Read from the Torah	❏	❏	❏	❏	_____
Lead prayers at synagogue	❏	❏	❏	❏	_____
Go to college	❏	❏	❏	❏	_____
Become a doctor	❏	❏	❏	❏	_____
Become a teacher	❏	❏	❏	❏	_____
Stay home to raise children	❏	❏	❏	❏	_____
Become a Rabbi or Cantor	❏	❏	❏	❏	_____
Work for tzedakah causes	❏	❏	❏	❏	_____
Light Shabbat candles	❏	❏	❏	❏	_____
Wear a kipah and tallit	❏	❏	❏	❏	_____
Do housework	❏	❏	❏	❏	_____
Learn to cook and/or sew	❏	❏	❏	❏	_____

One of those big adult choices is whether or not to raise a family. As you might imagine, Jewish tradition offers guidance on this matter. Here is Rabbi Hillel to share his teaching, along with three differing modern views on the subject. Check whether you agree or disagree with each one.

Hillel: The first commandment in the Torah is "Be fruitful and multiply." To me this means that every couple must have one son and one daughter to fulfill the mitzvah.
❑ **Agree**   ❑ **Disagree**

Have you noticed how crowded the world is getting? We don't need any more babies! That's why my partner and I adopted our kids. ❑ **Agree**   ❑ **Disagree**

Maybe the world is crowded, but there are so few Jews! And the Holocaust wiped out so many of us. Jewish families need to have many children to do God's mitzvot and to take care of each other. ❑ **Agree**   ❑ **Disagree**

I love my work! I might not marry or have children. I have lots of great friends and my dog Dreidel — and that's plenty for me. ❑ **Agree**   ❑ **Disagree**

CHECK IN > **What other things in a person's life might influence the decision to raise a family?**

_____

_____

Can you see how this might not be an easy decision?

It looks a bit cloudy and stormy here. Where are we?

Our Jewish tradition recognizes that people sometimes make mistakes. Not every marriage lasts forever. Therefore, there is a Jewish procedure for divorce.

DETOUR DIVORCE is like a big detour. It's a side road some of us will travel in our lives, as children and/or as adults. This side road may be quite bumpy and rocky, and not very scenic. Eventually, though, those of us who have been down this road will return to the smoother main road as we adjust to the changes in our lives following divorce.

Word Guide

Agunah – Literally "chained woman" – an Orthodox woman whose husband refuses to grant her a Jewish divorce

Get – Jewish divorce (document)

If the agunah *does* remarry, her children by that marriage will not be allowed to marry other Jews. Her ex-husband is free to remarry and have children. I ask you, is that fair?

CHECK IN

Complete the exercise below, whether or not you've been through the divorce of your parents. (If you haven't, try to imagine how it might feel).

Feelings about my parents' divorce:

I feel/felt sad because _____

I feel/felt afraid because _____

I feel/felt angry because _____

I feel/felt glad because _____

OLD AGE? How can we have gotten here so quickly? It seems as if we just left childhood . . .

A modern Rabbi wrote that:

> ❝ Old age is a blessing, a reward for living right, a time for special honor. ❞

> ❝ But it's also a time of loss, a time of illness and incapacity. ❞

Moving On

What might a person gain in old age?

_____

_____

What might a person lose?

_____

_____

MITZVAH STOP

Bikur Cholim (visiting the sick) is an important mitzvah, but it's not always an easy one to perform.

Have you spent time lately with an old or very sick person? How did you feel before, during, and after your visit?

_____

_____

_____

Oy! My knee is bothering me today. But you know what they say about getting old? It beats the alternative!

So here we are at the end of life. **DEATH** can be a difficult subject to approach. It can be scary and sad. Also, when we are young and healthy, a part of us might feel that death is very distant for us and our loved ones.

The truth is that death can occur at any time in a person's life — when we're young or old, healthy or sick.

Jewish tradition teaches that death and mourning are a part of life. Our tradition provides us with laws and customs to help us deal with these difficult times. So let's prepare ourselves by learning about this final landmark on our journey.

Word Guide

Aron – Casket. Jewish law states that it should be plain and made of wood.

Chevrah Kaddisha – Group of people who prepare a body for a Jewish burial

Hesped – Eulogy. A speech about the deceased is given at the funeral.

Kaddish – Prayer recited by mourners

K'riah – Tearing. Mourners tear a garment as a symbol of their grief.

Shivah – Seven. "Sitting Shivah" refers to the seven-day mourning period following burial.

Sh'loshim – Thirty. There is a thirty-day mourning period following burial.

Shomer – Guardian. A shomer stays with the body continuously from death until burial, as a sign of respect.

Tachrichim – Shrouds. These traditional burial garments are used to wrap the body.

Taharah – Ritual cleansing of the body after death

Yahrzeit – (Yiddish) Literally, "year time." Yearly anniversary of death. We observe the yahrzeit of a loved one by burning a 24-hour candle, giving tzedakah, and reciting Kaddish in the presence of a minyan.

Pretend you've just joined the local **Chevrah Kaddisha**. (Good for you! It's considered an honor.) You've been studying a set of cards with all of the Jewish rituals for death and burial. But the cards have fallen out of their case. They're mixed up, and some of the words are hard to read. Fill in the missing words, and put the cards in the right order by writing a number from **1** to **8** in the circle on each card.

Mourners and others take part in the mitzvah of throwing some _____ into the grave.

Finally, mourners recite the _____ prayer.

After the eulogy, the mourners _____ one of their outer garments. The _____ is lowered into the grave.

The funeral begins with the chanting of psalms and prayer, followed by a _____.

Place the body carefully into a plain wooden _____.

Make sure a _____ stays with the body from the moment of death until burial.

The body is ritually washed and dried. This is called _____.

After washing it, the body will be _____ in tachrichim.

The seven-day period of **shivah** begins immediately after the burial. Mourners gather at the home of the deceased (or one of the mourners). During this period, they grieve the loss of their loved one, remember and talk about him or her, and are comforted by friends and relatives.

There are many laws and customs pertaining to the shivah house. Match the probable reason on the right to the custom on the left.

____ Water, bowl, and towel are placed outside the door.

____ Services are conducted in the home.

____ Mourners don't watch television, listen to music, wear new clothes, shave, or use cosmetics.

____ Mourners sit on low benches or on a chair or sofa with cushions removed.

____ Mirrors in the house are covered.

____ Meals are served to the mourners by friends.

____ Meals may include eggs, lentils, garbanzo beans, and/or bagels.

____ The door is left unlocked, and visitors just walk in without ringing.

A. It is comforting to be taken care of by others.

B. Losing a loved one makes us realize we are humble (low) before the ways of God.

C. Mourners don't need to rise to greet visitors.

D. This gives mourners an opportunity to say Kaddish in a minyan.

E. These round foods remind us of the cyclical nature of life and death.

F. Mourners returning from the funeral ritually wash their hands.

G. Mourners need not worry about their physical appearance, and visitors will be reminded not to worry about everyday matters.

H. Mourners refrain from enjoyable or comfortable activities to focus on their loss.

Have you ever been to a shivah house (house of mourning)? If so, how many of the rituals described on page 49 did you observe? _____

CUSTOMS

We may honor the dead by giving tzedakah in their memory. Sending flowers for the funeral is *not* a Jewish custom.

A small bag of dirt from Eretz Yisrael may be placed in the casket along with the body.

A person may be buried in their tallit — but with the tzitzit cut off. Why do you think this is so?

_____

_____

CHECK IN

Look back at the Jewish customs for the treatment of a dead body (page 48). How do these practices help us to take part in the mitzvah of respecting the dead?

_____

_____

_____

It seems as if there are more Jewish practices concerning death and mourning than any other life cycle landmark. Why so many laws and customs?

How might sitting shivah help the mourners (and their friends) to express their grief and to heal?

_____

_____

_____

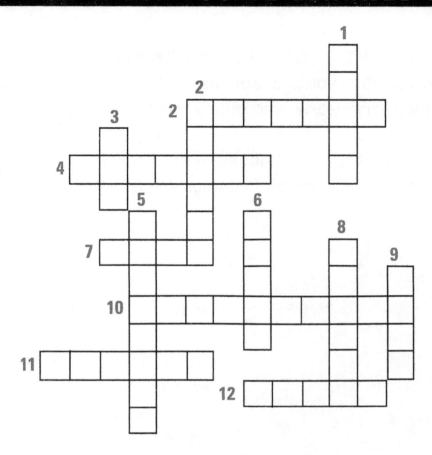

ACROSS

2. Bikur Cholim: the _____ of visiting the sick.

4. Pre-wedding veiling ceremony

7. _____ said to Naomi, "Your God will be my God."

10. To observe a yahrzeit, we light a candle that burns for _____ hours.

11. I've got the bride and groom covered.

12. Number of days for both a wedding feast and a house of mourning

DOWN

1. At the end of the wedding, I'm shattered!

2. No bubble bath allowed in the _____; it's for ritual purposes only.

3. Jewish divorce document

5. "Be fruitful and _____." (Genesis)

6. A shomer stays with the body from _____ until burial.

8. A ger or gioret is a Jew by _____.

9. This very plain box must be made of wood.

You'll find information for this crossword on pages 33 to 50.

OUR MAGIC CARPET JOURNEY has been long and full. If you're like most people, you probably remember some parts of the journey very clearly, and others hardly at all.

Don't get off that carpet just yet. You might need to go back to remind yourself of some of the things you learned.

Moving On

LIFE CYCLE LANDMARKS
BRIT = Brit Milah or Brit Bat
CONS = Consecration
MITZ = Bar/Bat Mitzvah
WED = Wedding
DIV = Divorce
D&M = Death & Mourning
CONV = Conversion

Below is a list of items associated with the "landmarks" (main events) of the Jewish life cycle. Write the code of the correct landmark next to each item. (There might be more than one code per line!)

_____ Ketubah	_____ Thirteen years	_____ Beit Din
_____ Naming	_____ Mikvah	_____ Agunah
_____ Chupah	_____ Taharah	_____ Tachrichim
_____ Sitting shivah	_____ Sandek	_____ Circumcision
_____ Wimpel	_____ Tiny Torah scroll	_____ Thirty days
_____ Haftarah	_____ Seven circles	_____ Get
_____ Broken glass	_____ Seudat Mitzvah	_____ Seven days

Let's further reflect on our travels by jotting down a few thoughtful observations — as any seasoned traveler might do after a long journey.

BIRTH/ADOPTION (pages 9-13)

I was interested to learn that _____

_____

I think the main idea behind our Jewish naming practices is

_____

_____

ENTERING THE COVENANT (pages 14-19)

I learned these three important words and their definitions:

1 _____

2 _____

3 _____

I think the purpose of celebrating Brit Milah or Brit Bat is

_____

_____

BEING A CHILD (pages 21-24)

Being a Jewish child means _____

_____

_____

BAR/BAT MITZVAH (pages 25-29)

I was surprised to learn that _____

_____

When I look forward to my Bar/Bat Mitzvah ceremony, I feel _____

because _____

_____

LOOKING BACK

GROWING UP (pages 30-31)

When I think about being a teenager, I look forward to _____

_____

I feel concerned about _____

_____

I will prepare for Confirmation by _____

_____

LEAVING HOME (page 33)

If I were to invent a Jewish ceremony for leaving home, I'd include

_____

_____

CONVERSION (pages 34-37)

I was interested to learn that _____

_____

I think the Jewish conversion process is meant to _____

_____

MARRIAGE (pages 38-42)

I learned these four important vocabulary words and their definitions:

1 _____

2 _____

3 _____

4 _____

My favorite Jewish wedding ritual is _____

because _____

_____

_____

BEING AN ADULT (pages 43-44)

I hope that as a Jewish adult I will _____

_____

_____

_____

DIVORCE (page 45)

I was interested to learn that _____

_____

Learning about divorce made me feel _____

_____

OLD AGE (page 46)

When I think about growing old, I feel _____

_____

because _____

_____

DEATH AND MOURNING (pages 47-50)

I learned these five important vocabulary words and their definitions:

1 _____

2 _____

3 _____

4 _____

5 _____

I think children ☐ should ☐ should not

be required to learn about death and mourning because _____

_____

_____

WELL, THAT'S IT. Be careful as you step off the carpet, back to your own life road.

Now that you, too, are a maven, Millie wants you to have these Flyer's Wings. But she can speak for herself — she always likes to have the last word, you know.

Listen, just because you're a big shot now, don't think it means you know everything about the Jewish life cycle. The good news is: you'll learn as you go! As you travel on your own life journey, you'll have books, Rabbis, teachers, and friends to teach you whatever else you need to know. I wish you a life full of joyous Jewish celebrations, and may our tradition also help you through the more difficult times.

Good luck, bubbeleh, and HAPPY TRAVELING!